FACET fb BOOKS

BIBLICAL SERIES — 1

John Reumann, General Editor

The Significance of the Bible for the Church

by ANDERS NYGREN

translated by Carl C. Rasmussen

FORTRESS PRESS   PHILADELPHIA

Copyright © 1963 By Fortress Press
Library of Congress Catalog Card Number 63-17879
ISBN 0-8006-3000-9

Second Printing 1965
Third Printing 1967
Fourth Printing 1976

5820D76   Printed in U.S.A.   1-3000

Introduction

I⟨T⟩ is no accident that current interest in the Bible and the revival of biblical theology go hand in hand with renewed emphasis on the church generally and with the movement toward reunion of the churches. For the Scriptures and the organized Christian community have always stood in close relation, either as rivals ("Shall the Book or the institution and its officials dominate?") or as allies, with Bible and church interpenetrating in believers' lives. Today we live in a period not only of interest in but also of debate about Bible and church.

Few men are able to speak on this topic with such depth of theological insight and breadth of practical concern as Anders Theodore Samuel Nygren, pastor, scholar, and churchman. Born in 1890 in Gothenburg, Sweden, he studied at Lund, the ancient university town and bishop's seat, with which his career has been closely associated. A parish minister in the Lutheran Church of Sweden from 1912 to 1920, he then began teaching at Lund where, in 1924, he was made a professor in the theological faculty. His early work was in the area of philosophy of religion, his chair in systematic theology, and his lectures and publications sometimes in the biblical field. Over the years Dr. Nygren has been active ecumenically, first in the Faith and Order and the Life and Work movements and then in the World Council of Churches.

61369

Within his own household of faith he served as the first president of the Lutheran World Federation (1947-52) and was made bishop of Lund in 1949.

His major literary work is a study of the two Greek words for love, which Nygren sees as rival motifs throughout the whole history of Christianity: *Agape and Eros*—a book so significant that it has been translated even into Japanese and Chinese! His *Commentary on Romans* is a major theological analysis of Paul's most important epistle, and reflections of Nygren's exegesis appear in the present work. In recent years he has continued to write and lecture, and his published volumes in English, often of a more general nature and intended for lay people, include *The Gospel of God, Christ and His Church*, and *Essence of Christianity*. Now retired, he is currently at work on a book on the philosophy of religion.

Amid the present debate about the Bible, inside as well as outside the church, three of the most pressing matters are those dealt with in the chapters of this book: (1) the relation of the Bible to revelation and to tradition; (2) the relation of the Old Testament to the New; and (3) the relation of critical, scientific scholarship to the practical, devotional interests of the average Bible reader. Dr. Nygren unfolds in simple, lucid terms the case (1) for the Bible as a message about God's dynamic acts and as a continuation of that action, available ever and afresh; (2) for both the newness and the continuity of the New Testament, so that there is a Christian as well as a strictly historical way of viewing the Old Testament, yet a way that is not allegory; and (3) for the historical-critical method of biblical study as a necessity, not a menace, for the life of Mr. Average Christian.

To a great extent this material has been developed in the course of lectures to, and actual encounter and discussion with, amateur and professional theologians, Christian lay people, and non-believers throughout the world. Chapter 1, on "Revelation and Scripture," stems originally from an address on "The Holy Scriptures and the Witness of the Church at the Present Day" given at an ecumenical conference in Bossey, Switzerland, in January, 1947, on "Biblical Authority for the Church's Social and Political Message Today." The address appeared in abbreviated form in the mimeographed report of the conference prepared by the Division of Studies of the World Council of Churches, *From the Bible to the Modern World* (pp. 51-53), and in the printed German account, *Der Weg der Bibel zur Welt* (pp. 79-83). In *Biblical Authority for Today* (edited by A. Richardson and W. Schweitzer), Nygren's contributions to the ecumenical discussion on this subject are noted. All three chapters of the present volume were presented in lecture form to American audiences during Bishop Nygren's months as visiting professor at The Ecumenical Institute, in Evanston, Illinois, and at the University of Minnesota in 1961.

For further reading, the book by Dr. Nygren's fellow professor at Lund, Ragnar Bring, *How God Speaks to Us: Dynamics of the Living Word*, is helpful. It was originally presented as lectures during a visit to America and reflects the Lundensian view of the Word of God as related to Bible and church. More details about the books mentioned above will be found at the end of the book.

Lutheran Theological Seminary   JOHN REUMANN
Philadelphia
June, 1963

In preparing a third printing of this Facet Book, the Editor is pleased to report that Professor Nygren's book on the philosophy of religion was recently announced for publication under the title *Meaning and Method in Theology and Philosophy*. To the bibliography at the end of this book have been added several titles dealing with the methodology of Professor Nygren over the years, notably a splendid introductory article in *The Expository Times* for July, 1963, by Philip S. Watson, who has done so much to introduce Lundensian thought and "motif-research" to Anglo-Saxon readers.   J. R.
January, 1967

Contents

REVELATION AND SCRIPTURE

WHAT is it that gives the Bible its decisive significance for the Christian life? It is the fact that it is God's word to us and that we here meet God's revelation. When we speak about the Bible we must consequently always speak about revelation at the same time.

REVELATION

The first thing that is necessary is to examine more closely what revelation is, in the Christian sense of the term. It happens very often that the concept is used in a sense quite other than the original Christian meaning. We have to distinguish between two different ways of viewing revelation: (1) the biblical, realistic, active concept, and (2) the intellectualistic concept, which came as a heritage from Greek thought and has held sway for the most part ever since the Enlightenment. When revelation is spoken of, and said to be contained in the Bible, we are prone to think that God was hidden at first. He concealed himself behind a veil, and man could neither know him nor know what he is like. And then came revelation, the drawing aside of the veil, disclosing him who had been hidden behind it. Now God is no longer unknown to man. Henceforth man knows him and his attributes. Man has a knowledge now that he formerly lacked. Such is the intellectualistic concept of revelation. People sometimes say that existence becomes transparent; something of God shines through, in nature, in human life, in history. We get a glimpse of the God who is hidden behind nature, the facts of conscience, and the destinies of history; but we see him chiefly in sacred history, and above all in the figure of Christ himself. In all this is the implication that the divine which is hidden behind things shines through the veil made transparent; and this is revelation: revelation in nature, revelation in conscience, revelation in history, revelation in Christ.

When the Bible speaks of revelation its meaning is quite different. We may give two examples, one from the Old Testament and one from the New. In Isaiah 52:10 we read, "The Lord has bared his holy arm before the eyes of all the nations." And Isaiah 53:1 asks, "To whom has the arm of the Lord been revealed?" This is a striking expression of the biblical concept of revelation. Revelation means that God enters in, lays bare his arm, and deals with us. Revelation is an active intervention of God. God does not sit still as the passive object of our observation. In revelation he is dealing actively with our existence, laying his hand on it and changing its circumstances. In this connection it may be interesting to recall one of the characteristics of the history of art, to which attention has often been directed. During the earliest Christian times men held firmly to the prohibition of images or likenesses. Hence there are no graphic representations of God from that age. When people wished to present a likeness of God, they showed "the arm of God." That is the way in which God reveals himself to us men. "Underneath are the everlasting arms" (Deut. 33:27). That presents the biblical concept of revelation.

And now we turn to the New Testament illustration, in Rom. 1:17. This is the extraordinarily important statement which serves as theme and summary for the whole epistle. Here Paul says, "The righteousness of God is revealed through faith for faith; as it is written, 'He who through faith is righteous shall live.'" The righteousness of God is revealed! There again is the concept of revelation. Closer examination of this passage discloses to us the meaning of the Christian concept, in contrast with the intellectual and static view.

In this brief verse the apostle has brought together four extraordinarily important concepts: gospel, righteousness, revelation, and faith. It is striking to note how the intellectualistic, static view of revelation has been able to construe these terms according to its own presuppositions, thereby giving them a meaning quite different from Paul's. For instance, the word "gospel" has been interpreted as if it meant only a doctrine or the proclamation of timeless religious truths. "The righteousness of God" is presented as a static attribute in the divine nature. "Revelation" is thought of as the theoretical communication of formerly hidden knowledge. And by "faith" is meant the affirmation and acceptance of this doctrine, of such universally valid religious ideas.

But one must discard that static and intellectualistic view at every point, if he would understand Paul. Not a fiber of its roots must remain. "The gospel" is not merely the proclamation of certain ideas, but—as the preceding verse (1:16) says—a divine dynamic, "the power of God for salvation," by which he snatches the victims of sin and death from their thralldom and brings them into the new relationship of righteousness and life. "The righteousness of God" is not a static attribute of God, but his mighty intervention in our existence, resulting in a complete change in its conditions. "The righteousness of God" is an *actuality* which he has effected in our midst, through Christ. In verse 18 Paul says that "the wrath of God is revealed from heaven against all ungodliness and wickedness of men." That is an actual and potent fact. And the righteousness of God in the new age is just as real and potent. When Paul says that this righteousness is "revealed," he is not thinking of revelation as an intellectual enlightenment. His concept of revelation is not intellectualistic and static. His concept, like that of the Old Testament, is *dynamic*—a divine dynamic, a power of God takes a hand in our existence.

Revelation is an action originating in God. Paul does not

start from a view of God as unknown, hidden from us by a veil. He does not think of revelation as a parting of a concealing veil, so that man may come to know what God is like, that God is righteous. Revelation is rather the mighty manifestation of God's will—at one time of his wrath, and at another of his righteousness. Just as the wrath of God comes down from heaven on the ungodliness of men, so too the righteousness of God has come down from above through Christ and is given to everyone who has faith in him. And "faith" is not merely an intellectual assent to the ideas of the gospel; it is rather the fact of being laid hold of and constrained by the power of the gospel, and thereby borne into the new age of life with Christ.

THE BIBLE

Revelation is the action of God, coming to its highest culmination in the fact that he sent Christ into our world and thereby bestowed his righteousness on us. But what is the Bible, then? It is both the message of that action and its continuation. A message is indeed an objective proclamation, announcing that something has happened; but it is more than that. In the message there is something of a transforming character; the message comes to be a continuation of the action, being, as it were, a very part of it. A convenient illustration may help.

In the Second World War, Denmark and Norway were occupied by Nazi troops. One day in May, 1945, came the message, "Denmark is free! Norway is free!" That news was a message in the most proper sense of the term. And it was also a message to us in Sweden because we had recognized the tragic lot of kindred peoples as our concern too. But when two hundred years hence men read about the liberation of those lands, that history will no longer have the character of a message. It will then be simply the repetition of an objective historic fact. What does it mean that it first came as a message? Primarily it means that something real had come about. But it also means that that which was reported was of crucial importance for him who heard of it. A power mightier than the invading enemy had come and deprived the foe of his sway. That was the objective fact. But by that fact the subjective situation of every individual had been mightily changed. They who before had been driven underground by fear of the conqueror could now come forth. Their law which had been pushed aside could again function. The time of arbitrariness and disregard of law was past. Man could breathe again and begin to live.

In such a case one can easily see how the objective and the subjective are bound up together. If the objective fact had not happened, if a greater power had not come and put down the usurper, all would have remained as it was; force, lawlessness, and fear would have continued to hold sway. There would have been no basis for a new message; for the message can proclaim only what has actually occurred. But—and now we see the other side of the situation—as long as the message about what has happened has not reached him who is in prison or in hiding, it is, for him, as if nothing had happened. He continues to live in fear and constraint. Life wears its old aspect, and tyranny still holds power. Only after the objective victory has been won and the message thereof has gone forth over the land do the fetters fall and the fears vanish; only then can one return to a life worthy of man. The change in the objective situation brings change in the subjective; or—as it might be better to say—it brings an objective change in the status of the individual. He can say, "The restoration of my country's freedom has restored my freedom too."

This illustration is not just a vague analogy with the fact of the Christian message. There is an actual correspondence. Our human life is by nature a life under alien powers. How that came to be, we may not be able to see clearly; but that it is so is a manifest fact. If we did not know that before, recent years have made it evident. Humanity has done everything to destroy itself. Men have literally poured down death on each other. Man has turned his back on God, and we see what his situation really is. How realistically the Bible judges man when it says he stands under the dominion of sin and death! Sin is the common guilt of the race, and we all share it. Sin is not—as men are prone to think—just certain moral failures for which we must bear the responsibility. Sin is a mighty power which holds us and all our race in its grip. When one gives himself to sin, he likes to think he is master of his own action, and that another time he can do good if he chooses. But that is an illusion. He who sins is the bond-slave of sin. Man is not master over sin; sin is master over him. By nature we stand with the whole race under this terrible dominion. Only a superficial view can hold that man can do good or evil as he chooses. It is about as if one said to one who lives in a subjugated country, "It is entirely up to you and your own volition whether you live in freedom or under oppression." Much does indeed depend on our choice. When we act against God's will, we cannot excuse ourselves, saying that we had no choice, that we were constrained against our will. On the contrary, when sin takes possession of a person, it does so by possessing his will, with the result that he sins willingly. And yet it is not in the power of our choice to decide whether we shall be sinners or not. It was not our choice that made us members of our sinful race. We were born into that relationship. Nobody inquired about our wishes or asked for our consent. And because of sin the race stands under God's condemnation. We live under a condemning law and under death. The wrath of God, sin, the law, death—in these four terms the epistle to the Romans describes the terrible powers of destruction that rule over man's life.

To us who live in the realm subjugated by sin, condemnation, the law, and death, God now proclaims his message: in Christ God has made a new beginning for our race. He has made Christ the head of a new humanity. By belonging to him all who believe in him are freed from all these forces of destruction. They are free from the wrath of God, not through their own accomplishment, but through Christ's atonement. They are free from sin, not in the sense that they rise above moral failure, but in the sense that sin is no longer their master; they are subject to another Lord, Jesus Christ. And in the same sense they are free from the law and from death. That is the central meaning of the gospel as Paul presents it in Romans, chapters 5-8. The great transformation from sin to righteousness, from the law to grace, from death to life, took place when God sent Christ into this lost world and when Christ gave himself for us. That is the great objective thing that has happened.

Thereupon many have reasoned as follows: If this has actually happened, if atonement has been made once for all, if release from the powers of destruction has been won, nothing further is necessary. The status of the human race has been changed; and in that change we share as members of the race. But such conclusions are entirely wrong.

It is true that from beginning to end salvation is an objective fact which God effected through Christ. But this is not an objective drama, in the sense that it happens without us. What would be the result for one who had been driven underground, if he never heard that his land had been freed or if he did not trust the report? That would not undo the fact that liberation had come; but he himself would have no part in it. He would go on hiding. He would always live under the old fear, subject to the power that had actually lost its power and authority over him. That is the reason why the word of God comes to us, not merely as a universally valid doctrine, but as a *message*, as a word directed personally to him who hears it. God has acted through Christ. If I believe, I share in what he has effected; if I do not believe, I do not share, and it means nothing for me.

What we have said can be summarized concisely as follows: *Revelation* is the activity of God, his active and effective intervention in human life. It reaches its height in God's action in Christ. The *Bible* is the *message* about this action; but *this message is itself an action of God*. When it is proclaimed, the fact is that God continues and completes his action in us. When the gospel is preached, God releases men from the dominion of the powers of destruction and makes them members of a new humanity whose Lord and head is Christ.

REVELATION AND SCRIPTURE

There is still another point to which we must give attention. In speaking of the Bible as the message about God's action, we have thought of that message as an actual proclamation. It is a message which comes from the living God; and it is directed to men now living, in whom God would effect his work. But now that message is written into a book, in Holy Scripture. The message is written in fixed form. This too is due to the character of the divine revelation.

With this we come to the final aspect of our problem: revelation and *Scripture*. We inquire what it means that the Christian revelation is preserved in fixed documents. Is Christianity really "a book religion"?

To this question a negative answer has often been given. It is said that only a lower form of religion can consider itself bound by a book and by unchanging scriptural documents, and that a more spiritual religion rises above that level. Not infrequently, in this connection, reference is made to the apostolic declaration, "The written code kills, but the Spirit gives life" (II Cor. 3:6). The idea is that Christianity, the religion of the Spirit, cannot be bound by the word of the Bible, by the "letter" (KJV) or "written code" (RSV) of Scripture.

But it is at once clear that Paul's words can be so understood only if they are misunderstood. When he speaks of the written code that kills, he is referring to the law, whose God-given function it is to lay low and to condemn to death. And when he speaks of the Spirit who gives life, he is referring to the gospel, to the word about Christ, and not to any human spirituality apart from the word. The suggested view is also entirely wrong as to fact. For there is actually no contradiction between the Spirit and the word. They belong together inseparably. It is through the word and only through the word that the Spirit is given to us. This tie with the word is so far from bondage to the external letter or written code that, on the contrary, it is the Christian's charter of liberty, as we shall explain.

In this connection we can see how false is the indictment which, ever since the Enlightenment, has been made against the Reformation's bondage to the word of Scripture. People have reasoned as follows: It was the great accomplishment of the Reformation that it broke definitely with the external authority of the pope and the church; but it made the mistake of substituting another external authority, the word of the Bible. So one could actually ask whether, after all, Roman Catholicism was not in some ways closer to the truth, because its authority is at least a living authority which can adjust itself to changing times; but the church of the Reformation bound itself to the changeless word of a book, and thus doomed itself to the rigidity of a dead orthodoxy. Therefore, just as the Reformation freed the church from one external authority, we must now go on to free it from the authority of the Bible. We must push on to the free religion of the Spirit, in which man is bound only by his own inner spirit.

That line of reasoning makes sense only on the basis of a definite presupposition that the task of the Bible is to convey universally valid religious truths, which man could as well—or better—bring forth from the depths of his own conscience. If the Bible's mission is rather to communicate a *message* to us, the situation is entirely different. When someone brings me a message, what can it mean if I say that, to reach the truth, I must free myself from all such external influences and occupy myself only with my own thoughts and spirit? It is through the word of him who brings me the message, and only by means of it, that I come into contact with the fact of which his word speaks.

The fact is that the Christian faith builds on a divine action which happened at a certain, concrete point in the history of our race. That divine act becomes a living reality in the present when the message about it comes to man and is received in faith. Every new generation must establish contact with that divine action, and it is precisely through the living message that such contact is possible. That message goes on from generation to generation, binding them all to God's work in Christ on which all rests. The message has been borne forward from generation to generation.

However significant such an unbroken tradition is, it suffers two limitations. It is in danger of being impoverished, and of becoming rigid.

Everything passed on by tradition is subject to gradual dilution and paling. That is particularly true of religious tradition, especially the Christian tradition. God's work in Christ and the message thereof is too tremendous for any generation to grasp its total meaning. Any age succeeds in grasping only a part of this message. Much is passed over without being understood or used. A generation can pass on as living tradition only that which it has itself been able to appropriate and make vital. If each generation had nothing more to draw on than the tradition which its predecessor passed on, progressive impoverishment would be inevitable. The result would be the continual dilution of the message. One generation could not grasp as its own all that was meaningful for another. But in Scripture every generation has access to one and the same divine word. On the pages of the Bible the Christian message in its original form shines forth for all who go to it. Every generation can stand immediately before the divine message. We are not dependent on the limitations in the understanding of previous ages. We have access to the message itself, for it is preserved for us in the Scriptures. It can speak to us immediately, even as to men in any other age. If the Christian is bound by the message of Scripture, that fact also means that he is free from the arbitrariness of men's interpretation of that message.

We have said that tradition is also liable to the danger of rigidity. Any age's understanding of the message is at least in part conditioned by the dominant cultural conditions. There is an inevitable connection between such conditions and the message, but as cultural conditions change, little by little, the earlier interpretation lingers on. Because circumstances have changed, the inherited view is not a living message to the new day. It becomes a rigid dogmatic formulation. But every age has a right to stand immediately before the Christian message, and not merely before a view of it which has been handed down from a past age. So history shows how liberation from a hardened tradition has generally come from immediate recourse to the Scriptures. Tradition is conservative. Scripture releases reforming powers for the renewal of Christianity.

2

THE OLD TESTAMENT IN THE
NEW COVENANT

Ever since the earliest days the church has seen the word of God in the unity of the Old and New Testaments. It is the same God who speaks in both. As "in many and various ways God spoke of old to our fathers by the prophets," so "in these last days" he has spoken in an entirely new way, through Christ (Heb. 1:1-2) and his apostles. The Bible, the unity of the witness of the Old and New Testaments, is the church's document on which all rests. Stress is laid on the fact of the unity of both testaments. The one is as much the word of God as the other. Only by taking both together (as *sacra scriptura cum veteris tum novi testamenti*) is the Bible the *judex, norma, et regula*, the rule and standard by which all doctrines are to be judged (Introduction to the Formula of Concord). The continuity between the Old and New Testaments is self-evident. They do not conflict.

Nevertheless, without in any way giving up that continuity, that oneness between the two testaments, it is quite clear, on the other hand, that something entirely new was inaugurated in Christ. Through the earthly life of Jesus Christ, through his death and resurrection, an alteration has been made in man's existence, so that man lives under conditions wholly different from those which obtained before the coming of Christ. Christ comes, not merely as the greatest in a series of prophets, but as the Son, as the author of a new age, as the head of a new humanity. This, too, is a self-evident proposition for the Christian faith.

There is really no tension at all between these two apparently opposite affirmations—the complete unity and continuity between the Old and New Testaments, on the one hand, and the utter newness of that which entered with Christ, on the other hand. This was clearly seen in Christianity's classic period. Paul knew that God allowed something incomparably new to enter through Christ; but he was none the less certain that "the law and the prophets" bear witness to Christ. Luther agrees entirely, and so in general do the other Reformers.

But there has been a significant change in attitude in recent centuries. The rise of the historical-critical study of the Bible has raised questions about the relation between the testaments. As long as men could, like Paul and Luther, see the New Testament in the Old there was no special problem. Christ stood there as the dominating, new fact which first made clear the true meaning of all that went before, as the central point to which everything in the Old Testament pointed, and from which all that followed came forth. Here there was room both for the tremendous new fact that came through Christ and for continuity with that which had preceded. But, as we said, biblical research made a striking change. The Swedish exegete, Olof Linton, has thus characterized the new situation:

Much has happened in the field of biblical research since Luther's day. Luther looked at the entire Bible from the viewpoint of the gospel and of faith in Christ; that which came later shed its light on what had gone before. But the newer research has rejected that principle. For the interpretation of a text appeal may be made only to contemporary and earlier texts. Not only is the interpretation of the New Testament freed from the later conclusions of the church; but the interpretation of the Old Testament is freed from New Testament concepts. Indeed all texts must be understood without reference to later texts. Each text must speak for itself. The traditional *interpretatio christiana*, which made Old Testament texts subordinate to those of the New, is broken down.[1]

[1] *Svensk Teologisk Kvartalskrift*, XIX (1943), 220-21.

Thus when biblical criticism faces the question of the relation between the Old Testament and the New, the result may be said to be the direct opposite of the earlier Christian view, as held by Paul and Luther. Two points stand forth distinctly when biblical criticism answers the question of the relation between the two testaments. First, there is the manifest tendency to reduce the new element that entered with Christ. That which is seen in Christ was already present in the Old Testament, though perhaps as a preparatory stage or a promise. It is the same as that which we find in Christ, though now in full form. But, in the second place, there is the insistence that the Old Testament must not be interpreted in the light of the New. It is held that to do so leads to errors just as wide of the truth as were later arbitrary, allegorical misinterpretations of the Bible. Rather, the Old Testament must be given a purely historical interpretation. Then it will be clear that its meaning is quite different from that to which Paul and Luther came by viewing the Old Testament in the light of the New. There it is—both ways! The Old Testament and the New are so *alike* in content that Christ does not bring in anything so extremely new! The two testaments are quite *unlike;* for the Old Testament is primarily concerned with other things, not with Christ!

One sees immediately that these conclusions flatly contradict each other. For Paul and Luther that which unites the testaments is precisely the tremendous new thing which Christ introduces. In him God's wonderful intervention comes to us in such dimensions that even what God did before the coming of Christ can be understood only in the light of this new action. God acted as he did in Old Testament days just because he would, in the fulness of time, do what he did through Christ. For the historical exegete (Bultmann, for example) Jesus is essentially a rabbi in the line of rabbis or prophets. He merely gives clearer point to that which is already found in them. It was the early church that held him to be something different. The unity between the testaments, for this view, lies in the fact that they are on the same plane and contain about the same message, differing only in degree.

Let us say here that insistence on a consistent, historical study of the Old Testament is fully justified and necessary. When the scholar undertakes to interpret an Old Testament statement — for instance, a word of prophecy — he wants to know what the statement meant to the prophet himself in his historical situation, and what it meant to the people of his own day, to whom he was primarily speaking. As an Old Testament exegete, the scholar does not ask himself what use the New Testament later made of the statement. That is not relevant to his task. If, for example, he expounds the original meaning of Hab. 2:4, "the righteous shall live by his faith," he must not derive his explanation from what Paul said about that text. It would not be right to assert that because Paul interpreted the text in a certain way, it therefore meant the same to the prophet. Here the principle quoted from Linton is in order: "For the interpretation of a text appeal may be made only to contemporary and earlier texts." One must understand every text "without reference to later texts. Each text must speak for itself." The historical inquiry must be carried through without deviation. The introduction of other considerations must be carefully avoided. It will not do to confuse the issue by appeal to "spiritual" exegesis. In a given historical situation the author spoke with definite, concrete meaning. If we would understand him, we must confine our investigation rigorously to the historical situation.

So far so good. But if the exegete therefore draws the conclusion that Paul was wrong when he let what had taken place through Christ shed its light on the Old Testament, or that Luther was wrong when he "looked at the entire Bible from the viewpoint of the gospel and of faith in Christ," it is the exegete himself who is in error. He would be right only on the assumption that Paul and Luther meant to set forth what the original, historical meaning was. But the fact is that they intended something quite different. For them the question was not what the prophet had said in his own historical setting, but what *God* wanted to say through the prophet.

We do not mean to suggest a contradiction between what the prophet or another Old Testament author said and what God intended to say. God meant to say just what the Old Testament prophet said. The prophet was not just talking by himself. He was not merely giving utterance to his own thoughts and speculations; he could truly say, "Thus saith the Lord." God sent the prophet to speak. And even if one attends only to the historical meaning, he hears what God meant to say. When the contemporaries of the prophet heard him and understood the literal significance of his words, they heard what God meant to say to them. We are not justified in saying they were mistaken. At that time God meant to be understood just so. But even at the time God knew to what use he would put the prophetic word, in the fulness of time.

There is a New Testament declaration which affirms this strikingly and clearly. First Peter 1:10-12 says, "The prophets who prophesied of the grace that was to be yours searched and inquired about this salvation; they inquired what person or time was indicated by the Spirit of Christ within them when predicting the sufferings of Christ and the subsequent glory. *It was revealed to them that they were serving not themselves but you, in the things which have now been announced to you*" (italics added). The words of Scripture are not addressed only to those to whom they were first spoken. Their meaning is not exhausted by what the prophet and his age saw in them. The prophets did not live in the fulness of time. It was not God's intention that *all* should be open and manifest before their eyes. But now the Scriptures are given to us also who live in the fulness of time. When the prophets looked forward and declared what the Lord would some day do, they were serving us by so doing. The prophets set forth the doings of the Lord which we know and experience. We understand better than the prophets what God has done, for we have seen the fulfilment. But without the aid of their words we should not have understood. It is only by searching the Scriptures that our eyes are open to the promise and its fulfilment.

The case can be expressed simply as follows. If one would understand what the Old Testament author meant by a certain statement, he must let the text speak for itself and interpret it with the aid of earlier or contemporary texts. That principle of interpretation is oft repeated and quite correct. It is right for the exegete to follow it, for his task is of course to determine the concrete, historical meaning of the text. In his role as Old Testament scholar this is his only task. But when we turn to the Pauline writings we see that Paul's purpose is quite different; and the same is true of Luther. They do not ask what the human author meant or what God meant to say to the prophet's age. They do ask what God means to say, through those words, to us now in the time of fulfilment. The problem which occupies them is not historical, but, properly speaking, theological. Paul believes that God has, in a wholly unique way, entered into human history and revealed himself in Jesus Christ. This new act of God sheds light on all God's earlier acts and words. These we see in a wholly new light. Paul says that it is only through Christ that the veil is taken away, so that the deepest meaning of the Old Testament is no longer hidden (II Cor. 3:14). Only through Christ can we understand what God meant and what he would say to us through the words of the Old Testament.

If we are to avoid confusion, we must from the very start see clearly that there are two quite distinct, inescapable, and proper ways of understanding the Old Testament: the purely historical view and the view that rests on the New Testament. This double meaning is in a certain sense rooted in the very nature of the case. We must be careful not to let the one approach to Scripture blunt and override the other. On the one hand, we must not say that, since God meant the prophetic word to say to us Christians that which Paul sets forth, it is therefore wrong to give serious attention to the word's original, historical meaning. But on the other hand, it is quite as unjustifiable to hold that, since the word's historical, original meaning can be shown, it is wrong to follow the example of Paul and Luther, inquiring as to God's further meaning and what the prophetic word has to say to us who view it in the light of its fulfilment.

In this matter the school of critical biblical research has often been the aggressor. Probably no one can challenge the characterization by Olof Linton, cited above, of the position of the newer scholarship on this point: "Luther looked at the entire Bible from the viewpoint of the gospel and of faith in Christ; that which came later shed its light on what had gone before. *But the newer research has rejected that principle.*" But, one asks, is it really inadmissible to view the Old Testament from the viewpoint of the gospel and of faith in Christ? To be sure, to do so does not yield a historical-exegetical picture of Old Testament religion. If it is *that* which one seeks, this is certainly not the proper approach. But it was something quite different with which Paul and Luther busied themselves in their use of the Old Testament. Is it improper to inquire what the Old Testament means for those who believe in God's redemptive work in Christ, who believe, furthermore, that the work was envisioned in what God did in earlier times? One must ask what kind of scholarship it is which considers itself able to reject the interpretation of Paul and Luther, and to assert that God did *not* mean to say what they understood him to say. Such rejection would be in order only on the assumption that Paul or Luther says that his interpretation presents the historical meaning of the Old Testament expressions. That is by no means the case. Paul, for instance, distinguishes between the statement's literal, historical meaning and its deeper significance intended by God for the time of fulfilment. And as to Luther, his intention is made clear enough by a single representative declaration. Speaking about Paul's use of a statement in Deuteronomy, Luther says,[2] "Moses did not use this word with that intention. But the apostle, with his unsurpassably clear and

---

[2] See Luther's discussion of Deut. 30:12 in his commentary on Rom. 10:3-9; cf. *Luther: Lectures on Romans*, trans. and ed. Wilhelm Pauck ("Library of Christian Classics," Vol. XV [Philadelphia: Westminster, 1961]), p. 288.

spirit-filled insight, sets forth the very core of its meaning; for he shows us that Scripture everywhere speaks only of Christ, if one looks deeply, even though outwardly, and as far as it is a shadow, it sounds otherwise." Thus Luther shows that he understands very well that Paul is not attempting to set forth the simple, historical significance of a scriptural statement; but he is just as sure that Paul has set forth God's ultimate meaning, when the apostle views God's preparatory revelation in the light of his full revelation in Christ. Like Paul, Luther believes that there is a unity in revelation which can be understood only by seeing it whole. There is no responsible scholarship which can assert that his belief is false.

THE OLD TESTAMENT AND THE NEW

This is the question which confronts us: How does the New Testament view the Old Testament and its own relation to it? Is the New Testament only the ongoing of that which is already in the Old, a new stage in the Old Testament frame of divine fellowship? Or, if the New Testament introduces something new and on a higher plane, does it stand in a relation of continuity with the Old, or is the continuity broken? The answer to these questions must be found in the New Testament itself.

The first truth to be affirmed is that the New Testament is actually aware that it presents something absolutely new. The New Testament is characterized by a tremendous new note which must not be treated lightly. The secret which through all past ages (*chronois aiōniois*) remained untold has now been revealed through Christ (Rom. 16:25-26). The righteousness of God has now been revealed and made ours (Rom. 3:21). Now that Christ has come, the new aeon, the resurrection aeon, has come upon us. Now the last days have arrived. As in many and various ways God spoke of old to our fathers by the prophets, he has now in these last days, which Christ has ushered in, spoken to us in a wholly new way, through the Son, who is the reflection of the glory of

God and the Lord of all creation (Heb. 1:1 ff.). The New Testament testifies that in Christ God did something utterly new. The new aeon, which came to the world through Christ, is different in kind from the old. Through Christ the world and humanity now stand under wholly different conditions. That is true also of the relation of the New Testament to the Old. The great difference between the two is that in the Old Testament Christ had not yet come, while in the New he is in our midst. That is not a minor difference. In the Old Testament the pious died in faith, before they had received that of which the promise spoke, having only seen it from afar (Heb. 11:13). They had to be content with the foreshadowing of that which was to come; but for us who live in the last days God had foreseen something better, the fulfilment, the realization (Heb. 11:40). Christ "was destined before the foundation of the world but was made manifest at the end of the times" (I Pet. 1:20).

We get exactly the same concept from Jesus' own testimony in the gospels. John the Baptist was greatest in the old order. He came preaching that "the kingdom of heaven is at hand" (Matt. 3:2). But then when the kingdom of heaven had come through Christ, it could be said, "he who is least in the kingdom of heaven is greater than he" (Matt. 11:11). It was the extraordinary advantage of the disciples that they lived after the new had arrived, the coming of the messianic age. "Blessed are the eyes which see what you see! For I tell you that many prophets and kings desired to see what you see, and did not see it, and to hear what you hear, and did not hear it." (Luke 10:23-24, Matt. 13:16-17).

In Second Corinthians, chapter 3, Paul has given an exceptionally enlightening presentation of that which is new in the New Testament, in relation to the Old. Here the two covenants are presented in sharp antithesis—the new covenant (*hē kainē diathēkē*) and the old (*hē palaia diathēkē*). The old covenant is the ministry (RSV, "dispensation") of the law and the written code; and this is characterized as the ministry of death and condemnation (*hē diakonia tou thanatou, tēs katakriseōs,* 3:7, 9). The new covenant is the ministry of the Spirit and of righteousness (*hē diakonia tou pneumatos, tēs dikaiosunēs,* 3:8, 9). As to both covenants and their missions, it is true that they are of God. Therefore, though the law kills and condemns, it can be said that the ministry of the law is glorious (RSV, "with . . . splendor," 3:7). All that is of God is *doxa,* glory; the law is God's law, and as such it is holy and just and good (Rom. 7:12). There is no contradiction of this when it is said that the law kills and condemns; for it does this precisely as God's holy and just law. It is exactly the mission of the law to kill and condemn. That is God's intention and purpose for the law.

But the ministry of the law is to end; II Cor. 3:11 (RSV), it is "what faded away" (*to katargoumenon*). Its power was taken away when the new age came, the age of life through Christ. For Christ is the *telos* of the law—the "conclusion," the "end" of the law, unto righteousness for everyone who has faith (Rom. 10:4). The ministry of righteousness or of the Spirit takes its place. The antithesis between these two offices and the two testaments is manifest. The new sets a limit for the old and brings it to an end. A more direct antithesis is hardly conceivable. But is this an antithesis in the sense that one testament calls the other false? By no means! The law rightly expressed God's relation to mankind, and it expresses what is always his relation to man outside of Christ, apart from Christ. There is no contradiction in the fact that in the old aeon God placed mankind under the dominion of the law that condemns, and that through Christ he has now established an utterly new relation and placed those who are "in Christ" under the dominion of righteousness and life. "Therefore if any one is in Christ, he is a new creation; the old has passed away, behold, the new has come" (II Cor. 5:17). The law of condemnation and death also belongs to the old that has passed away. The Christian is free from that law, says Romans, chapter 7; and Rom. 8:1 sums up as follows: "There is therefore now no condemnation for those who are in Christ Jesus"; for there is for them no law that can condemn. The day of the law is past. We must beware lest, under the influence of Paul's positive attitude to Scripture and his appeal to the witness of "the law and the prophets," we blunt somewhat what he says about the law and the fact that it has been deprived of its dominion over those who are "in Christ" and have him as their Lord. But, on the other hand, it does not follow that there is any contradiction between the Old Testament and the New, between Moses as the central figure of the old covenant and Christ as the head of the new. The opposition, the contradiction, arises if, after Christ has been given to us, we continue under the dominion of the law, to which God fixed the frontier through Christ. For when God's new action in Christ came in its infinite glory, then, so to speak, 'the glory of that which had gone before came to an end (II Cor. 3:10).

Christ is the turning point in God's history with mankind. He makes all things new, absolutely new. He deposes the old powers, including the law. He outmodes the ministry of the law and death, so that it is henceforth called "the old covenant" which has been superseded by the new.

But when this has been made clear, we must, on the other hand, affirm that *the continuity between the two covenants and the two testaments is constantly maintained*. The whole Old Testament is carried over into the New. The Scriptures of the old covenant become the Scriptures of the new covenant, precisely because they bear witness to Christ and point forward to him. In this connection John 5:39 ought to be cited, to begin with. According to that passage Jesus says to the Jews, "You search the scriptures, because you think that in them you have eternal life; and it is they that bear witness to me." They who rightly understand the Old Testament find there a witness to Christ, for in the final analysis everything in the Old Testament looks forward to him. "To him all the prophets bear witness that every one who believes in him receives forgiveness of sins through his name" (Acts 10:43). The "searching of the Scriptures" therefore became a fundamental and essential part of the Christian's daily life. It was in that way that he was brought to faith in Christ and was confirmed in that faith. Acts recounts how Paul preached the gospel in Beroea and adds, "They received the word with all eagerness, examining the scriptures daily to see if these things were so. Many of them therefore believed" (Acts 17:11-12). Here is the reason for the "scriptural proof" of the earliest Christian theology. It was by viewing the new thing that had come through Christ in the light of what the Old Testament had written about him that early Christianity came to its understanding of God's new action.

It is clear from this that it was not only certain special parts of the Old Testament, the "messianic prophecies," which could be applied to Christ. *Everything* in the Old Testament was viewed as pointing forward to him. The acceptance of that conviction by early Christianity was utterly universal. To him all the prophets bore witness. The entire Old Testament without exception—both the law and the prophets—refers to Christ. To the disciples on the way to Emmaus Jesus says, "O foolish men, and slow of heart to believe all that the prophets have spoken!" "And," the record adds, "beginning with Moses and all the prophets, he interpreted to them in all the scriptures the things concerning himself" (Luke 24: 25, 27). "Moses and all the prophets" had borne witness of him. "In all the scriptures" reference is made to him. He is the special object of all the Scriptures. All Scripture revolves around him.

Under such circumstances it is only natural that throughout the Old Testament, predictions of Christ are seen. The declaration concerning the Suffering Servant (Isa. 53) is applied to Christ (Acts 8:32-35). As to the rock that yielded water to the children of Israel in the wilderness, Paul says, "The Rock was Christ" (I Cor. 10:4). The law and the prophets bore witness to the righteousness of God which was revealed in Christ (Rom. 3:21). The law itself testifies both against righteousness by the law and for faith in Christ. Abraham, the Old Testament patriarch, serves as the type and pattern of those who believe in Christ, of those who through faith are righteous (Rom. 4:23). In circumcision, the sign of the old covenant, Paul sees a sign and seal of the righteousness of faith which is revealed through Christ (Rom. 4:11). And probably the greatest illustration of how the Old Testament is regarded by the New is the fact that Paul takes as the theme of the letter to the Romans a declaration from the Old Testament, Hab. 2:4 (cf. Rom. 1:17).

To say it concisely, *everything* in the Old Testament is understood as pointing to Christ, in the relation of promise and fulfilment. All that is said in the Old Testament looks forward to the fulfilment in Christ. And, conversely, all which the New Testament says about Christ is regarded as already present in the Old Testament, at least in a preparatory way.

But now the question arises, how are these two ideas related—one, that something absolutely new has come through Christ, and the other, that all is already present in the Old Testament? Is there not a contradiction here? Does not the constant recourse to the Old Testament minimize the new thing that has come through Christ? No, quite the contrary is the case. Just because the New Testament is so convinced that in Christ God has given mankind a new beginning, it must see in *all* God's prior action a reference to his new action. We may refer again to Second Corinthians, chapter 3. Because Paul knows that it was in Christ that God spoke his final and decisive word, he also knows that the Old Testament cannot be rightly understood apart from Christ. Before Christ came a veil hung before the Old Testament, so that men could not understand its deepest meaning. Now that Christ has come, that veil is taken away, in principle. God has himself disclosed the deepest meaning, so that anyone may understand. But even though the veil has in principle been taken away through Christ, so that the Scriptures of the old covenant henceforth stand uncovered before us, nevertheless the veil still remains for those who do not believe. "To this day whenever Moses is read a veil lies over their minds; but when a man turns to the Lord the veil is removed" (II Cor. 3:15-16).

In Christ and only in him is the key given for the right understanding of the Old Testament.

Here a word must be added to guard against a likely but false statement of the problem of the attitude of early Christianity to the Old Testament. It might seem to us as if the Old Testament were a problem for early Christianity; as if it were only with difficulty and by all kinds of reinterpretations that the early Christians could come to terms with the testimony of the Old Testament. We think that Christianity had its fixed point of departure in God's new work in Christ; that it found difficulty in reconciling the earlier Old Testament revelation with the new one; and that the difficulty could be resolved only to the degree that it was possible to reinterpret the Old Testament statements in harmony with those of the New. For us, therefore, stress is usually laid on interpreting the Old Testament in the light of the New. For early Christianity, the problem was quite different. The Old Testament and its place constituted no problem. This was rather the accepted point of departure. To be sure, the Old Testament received its final interpretation in the light of that which had occurred through Christ; only by faith in him is the veil removed. In that sense the Old Testament does indeed get its interpretation through the New. But it is just as important to see that the new fact which had come in Christ can be correctly understood only in the light of the witness of the Old Testament. In this sense it can also be said that the New Testament gets its interpretation from the Old.

The Old and the New Testaments interpret each other mutually, and only by this mutuality does the Christian witness come into its right. As we have said, early Christianity came to its understanding of God's new action in Christ only by considering it in the light of what had been written about him in the Old Testament. It was not for Jews and Greeks alone that the affirmation about the crucified Christ was a stumbling block and foolishness. For the very disciples of Jesus the word of the cross was a hard paradox. That paradox could be resolved only on the thesis that in it "the foolishness of God" was manifest (I Cor. 1:21, 25). Here the Old Testament brought help. The difficulty was surmounted by pointing to "Moses and the prophets." Thus it could be said, "Was it not necessary that the Christ should suffer these things and enter into his glory?" (Luke 24:26). Otherwise the word about the cross remains an offense. God had himself given the prophecy in the Holy Scriptures. That which was apparently without sense, he had lifted up to a plane that gave it an absolute meaning. The paradoxical is no longer an offense. It rather expresses "the foolishness of God" which "is wiser than men" (I Cor. 1:25). Thus it is the Old Testament which supplies the key to the understanding of Christ. The work which God effected in Christ is not such as to supply its own interpretation forthwith. The New Testament is necessary to unveil the deepest meaning of the Old Testament; but it is just as necessary that God's work in Christ be seen in the light of the Old Testament, in order that its deepest meaning may be comprehended. It is hard to see how the preaching of Christ's death on the cross could have been effective had not the Old Testament declaration regarding the Suffering Servant been available (Isa. 53).

THE EXEGESIS OF PAUL

In the foregoing we have been occupied to a large extent with Paul's concept of the Old Testament. This has supplied the basis for a view of Paul's characteristic exegesis. Of what kind is it?

We can say at once that his exegesis does not depend on a passage's literal, historical meaning. It is safe enough to assert that, in general, he is familiar with the clear, literal meaning of the Old Testament passages. But that is not what interests him. What he looks for is types and references to that which God has now done in Christ. It is this, God's action in Christ, that he seeks to understand, and to that end he goes back to the Old Testament. It has often been held that his is an example of allegorical interpretation, in the usual sense of the word. Many have spoken of his enormous arbitrariness in exegesis. When it can be pointed out that in one place Paul himself characterizes his interpretation as "an allegory" (*hatina estin allēgoroumena*, Gal. 4:24), the case seems to be clear.

But if we speak here of an allegorical view, we ought to note that it is an allegorical interpretation very different from the usual kind. The characteristic of the allegorical method is its arbitrariness—in a double sense. On the one hand, it arbitrarily ignores the literal meaning; and on the other hand, it substitutes a meaning that is arbitrary and without rule. Usually a sensory experience is considered a symbol of psychological or spiritual experience, or a specific historical event is held to reveal an ideal relationship. The possibilities of that method of interpretation know no limits except fantasy; that is to say, there are no limits. A thing can mean practically anything. When one cuts loose from the historical meaning, interpretation drives before the wind.

If one compares Paul's interpretation of the Old Testament with this, he can say at once that there is a striking independence of the historical meaning of a passage. From a purely exegetical point of view, it is clear that Paul often interprets passages in a way quite different from the original, historical significance. But, then, Paul does not present himself as an exegete. His purpose is not to trace the literal, human meaning of the words. He asks what *God means to say to us* through them. And yet he does not allow himself to interpret them any way he pleases. God himself, by his new action in Christ, has interpreted his Old Testament word. Here is the principle by which Paul is absolutely bound in his understanding. The way in which God has given the fulfilment shows just how his earlier revelation is to be construed. Hence Paul can again and again permit himself a striking freedom from what the literal word says; but on the other hand, he is kept from arbitrariness by the fact that his interpretation is bound by a clear norm. He is not free to let his own fancy suggest what the Old Testament passage to be expounded may mean. God himself has supplied the interpretation through Christ; and by that Paul is bound. Here, in a new sense, one can use the words, "Christ is the end [*telos*] of the law" (Rom. 10:4). The whole Old Testament revelation points forward to Christ. He is the *telos* which God set for all his preceding revelation.

INTERPRETING THE BIBLE TODAY

Now we come to our final question: What does the above mean for our theological view of the Bible?

One thing is immediately clear. For a purely historical exegesis of the Old Testament we do not appeal to Paul. When the purpose is to arrive at a historical interpretation of a *particular Old Testament passage*, it would not be relevant to appeal to the fact that Paul understands it in this way or that, as if that settled the question of the original meaning. Paul never pretended that he was interpreting the Old Testament in this historical way. One therefore misuses Paul's word if he looks in it for the answer to such historical-exegetical questions. But this is only one point to be stressed with respect to the Old Testament. Our interest in the Old Testament is not limited to the exegete's historical interpretation of the original meaning. To the degree that the Old Testament is, so to speak, incorporated into the New, it is a matter of highest importance to note precisely how the New Testament interprets the Old. This is a vital point for our description of the New Testament's own outlook. But this, too, is a purely historical issue.

We go a step further when we ask how far, as a matter of principle, we ourselves, in formulating our theology, may make use of the view which the New Testament and Paul hold regarding the Old Testament. This question brings us back to the issue with which we started: Must we reject Paul's and Luther's concept of the Bible, according to which the *whole* Bible, including the Old Testament, is looked at from the viewpoint of the gospel and of faith in Christ? The answer to this question depends upon the answer to another: Do we really believe that God through Christ actually entered into a completely new relation to humanity? If we believe in the God who sent Christ into the midst of history and thereby gave our race a new beginning, then we cannot keep from looking at all things, *at all things without exception,* from that central point. That the Old Testament is included in our Bible is due to the fact that it is incorporated into the New Testament and has been colored by it, even as it has itself colored our understanding of the New Testament. As Christians we are interested in what Genesis says about Adam primarily because, with Paul, we see Adam and Christ in juxtaposition as type and antitype (*typos—antitypos*). In the figure of Abraham something essential is missed if he is not regarded as the father of the faithful (Rom. 4). And how could we as Christians read about the Suffering Servant of the Lord without seeing there him who "was wounded for our transgressions and bruised for our iniquities"? If we believe that Jesus is the Messiah-Christ, how could we follow the messianic thought through the Old Testament without seeing its culmination in Christ? On this point, the latest exegetical scholarship, by its emphasis on the dominant role of the messianic concept in the Old Testament, has made it easier to see the intimate relation between the two testaments. Similarly one could mention point after point in the Old Testament, and show that light has been shed on it by the New Testament, by Christ.

This is tantamount to saying that our theological interest can never be exhausted by a purely historical exposition of the Old Testament. That would be to impoverish Christianity unbelievably. Take out of the New Testament all that builds on an Old Testament foundation, and Christianity itself vanishes. We are reminded of that by the very name "Christianity," for that too builds on the Old Testament. In Acts it is reported that "in Antioch the disciples were for the first time called Christians [*christianoi*]" (11:26). "Christ" is of course the Greek translation of the Old Testament name "Messiah." The "Christians" are the new messianic congregation, which has received from God the fulfilment of the promises given in the Old Testament; they are the holy people of God gathered around his Messiah.

It is thus not a historical accident that the New Testament incorporates the Old into itself. If Christianity were but the proclamation of ideas, the earlier, Old Testament stage could have been left behind as outmoded. But Christianity is a message about a divine action, an action which loses its meaning if it is not coupled with what went before, as fulfilment of the earlier promise.

On the other hand, we must not tone down the difference between the Old Testament and the New, so that we see in the Old Testament only that which speaks directly of Christ, or refuse to see that in the new covenant God has through Christ given us something utterly new. It is not without purpose that God has given us his revelation in two testaments, in two covenants. God has not given the promise and the fulfilment in a single act. He has separated them as two distinct realities. We must not arbitrarily distort that relationship. Before the fulfilment in Christ, a veil hung before the Old Testament; and—we may add—it was God's intention that the veil should be there until the time when it pleased him to remove it, in the fulness of time. Thus for us Christians it is important to take the Old Testament with all seriousness, so that we see God's history with Israel in its own light, and not only in the light which Christ sheds on it once the veil has been removed. God is the God of history, who deals with every age in its own way. Only if we learn to see each of the testaments in its own character, do we give full weight to the double revelation which God has made in history. And in this the purely historical study of the Old Testament documents can give us valuable help.

In the fact that God has determined the relation of the two testaments as promise and fulfilment, he has both bound them together in a unity and differentiated them clearly from each other. Both facts are equally important. Once we see this relation and this unity, however, it is possible to overlook the difference. But the glory of God also manifests itself in the fact that the fulfilment came in a way quite different from what the people of promise had expected; and in looking for similarities we should not attempt to improve on God's history with Israel by reading back into it that which came only when the fulfilment arrived through Christ. We ought not to forget that it was at a definite point in history that the veil was removed. Because we live in a time when the veil has been taken away, we ought not to pretend that it was never there. That would be to falsify God's history with his people and to minimize what God has given us through Christ.

An analogy from the domain of the Christian life can make this clear. The whole of the Christian life is like a promise of something that *is to come*, a promise of the glory of God that *shall* be revealed. The Christian life stretches on toward the goal of the consummation. When that consummation arrives, it will be the fulfilment for which we as Christians have hoped and aimed. It can be said that now we both have it and do not have it. For when the fulfilment of our hope comes, it will be entirely different from what we have thought and imagined. "We are God's children now; it does not yet appear what we shall be" (I John 3:2). It would not be true to pretend that we already have all that is to be. That would be to seize in advance, and claim before the time, that which God intends to reserve for the next world.

God's history with mankind proceeds through three stages. In the old covenant he gave the promise of the Messiah; but a veil hides that which is to be, permitting only a foregleam. When fulfilment comes it is different in kind and of far greater glory than any in the old covenant could conceive. The second stage is the time of fulfilment. The time is fulfilled: Christ has come, the veil is removed. But a third stage is still to come: the consummation. As long as that stage has not arrived, there is still something toward which we must push on. Salvation has been bestowed on us; it is already ours, yet only in hope. We live in hope and not in seeing. We have God's promise of the glory that is to be, but a veil still conceals it, so that we cannot yet conceive precisely what the heavenly life will be like. Even when imagination draws a picture, we know the actuality will be quite different.

So those of an earlier day were right when they held that both Old Testament and New Testament are God's word. The Old Testament is indeed, in its literal, historical meaning, a record of God's history with his people in the time of the old covenant. But, besides that, it stands there pointing on to him who is to come, and by whom—now that he has come—the veil is removed and the deepest meaning of the Old Testameant is fully revealed. That meaning *is* the Messiah, Jesus Christ.

3

BIBLICAL RESEARCH AND THE PRACTICAL USE OF THE BIBLE

No other book in the world has received such thorough study or complete commentary as the Bible. Limitless labors have been given to the attempt to discover, from the best manuscripts we have, the earliest and the best text possible. No labor has been spared in dealing with the philological and historical issues that cluster about the text of Scripture. Scholars have drawn on all that could be known about the religion and culture of the world out of which the Bible came. The aim has been to understand the precise meaning of the Scriptures. Every verse in the Bible has received repeated expositions; and around some of those verses a whole literature has grown. Nor has scholarship been content to deal only with philological and historical issues. It has also dealt with questions of systematic and biblical theology. All the basic concepts of both Old Testament and New Testament have been defined and explored. When we deal with the Scriptures we are at work in a field which scientific study has cultivated in unique degree. It is to this whole enterprise that we refer when we speak of "biblical research."

How does it happen that it is the Bible to which such exceptional study is given? The answer to that question takes us into the area of practical religion. It is manifest that the reason for such intensive preoccupation with the Bible is its tremendous religious importance. That the Bible texts receive such minute philological and historical scrutiny is clearly not because they present problems in those areas which are so much greater than we can find in other writings; but behind all this scientific endeavor there lies the realization — more or less clearly seen—that the matter about which these texts speak is of such extraordinary importance for man that no labor is too great, if it can shed light even on a relatively subordinate point. The Bible has a mission to fulfil among men, and it is for the sake of this mission that research goes on and on.

A parenthetical observation may be in order here. It might seem that the scientific character of this research would be sacrificed to the practical end in view. But that need not follow. We have no right to use the term "biblical research" unless the study is theoretically unbiased and rigorously scientific. The sole object must be to attain an objectively true knowledge of what the Bible actually contains. It involves no interference with scientific, objective procedure when we note that behind that scientific treatment there lies a practical interest in the fact of which the Bible speaks. The opposite is rather the case. Precisely because the matter is of such decisive importance it is of supreme urgency that the truth be brought to light, the objective truth and nothing else. The scientific and the practical interests join in insistent demand for truth and objectivity.

But there is a problem here nevertheless. The Bible comes to us with the claim that it is *God's word*, through which he personally would speak to us. That inevitably affects our use of the Bible. We face the question, what can biblical research contribute to the end for which the Scriptures were given to us? We have said that by biblical research we mean the purely objective, scientific study which aims only at discovering what the content of Scripture actually is. Is such research really necessary for the practical use of the Bible? Or is it something which could be omitted without loss? Or is it perhaps actually a barrier to the practical use of the Bible? Are they right who say that, since it is God's word that comes to us in Scripture, we have only to accept it with the heart; that any attempt to submit it to objective scrutiny is a piece of human audacity which makes us deaf to what God says? This is the meaning of the problem of the relation between "biblical research and the practical use of the Bible."

Those who in the interest of the practical use of the Bible reject the critical study of it usually do so on the basis of a view that needs to be examined. They hold that the Bible is, in the first place, a book of worship and edification through which God speaks to our hearts and consciences. To speak of research and objective study of the contents of such a book is, it is said, to make it impossible for it to fulfil its purpose. When God speaks, it is our business to listen with folded hands and let his word do its work in our hearts. The attitude of research is here improper and out of place. It involves a denial of the divine character of Scripture, when men treat it like any human work which can be defined and tested objectively. God's word is not open to the curiosity of scientific inquiry, but only to humble hearts which use it in piety and prayer.

In such a view there is a mixture of both truth and falsehood. It is true that the word of God attains its purpose only if it reaches the heart and conscience of man; and that happens only when man receives it eagerly in prayer and obedience. But it is incorrect to think that this subjective effect is lost if one recognizes that the word has a definite objective meaning. That would be nothing less than, in the interest of a subjective piety, to turn away from what God actually says to us. That would be to treat God's word as if it had no meaning except what we subjectively read into it. Behind this view, as we have said, is hidden a false concept of the Bible and of the way it works. It assumes that the purpose of the Scriptures is to foster in us a certain attitude. It regards the Bible as we might appraise the effect of a poem or a musical composition on us. To state prosaically the meaning of a poem might rob it of its effect. Detailed analysis might point out clearly what the poem means; but it is often the elusive and the veiled in a poem which stirs feeling and fancy, and gives the work its depth and beauty. The same is true of music. There can be no exclusive interpretation of great music. Such music does not have the same effect on all who hear it, nor is that the intention. The great purpose is rather the subjective impression awakened within the individual. It is something like this which this false view of Scripture sees in the Bible. It is not concerned to discover the objective meaning; indeed it may definitely oppose the attempt. It holds that too clear a perception of the meaning of any context may rob the divine word of its aura, and therefore of the effect that aura gives it.

This view is guilty of a fatal oversight when it rests on the foregoing analogy. It fails to see that the Bible is a *message*, an objective message to us, a message about an action which God has effected for us. To what point does this statement now bring us? Has the rejection of the foregoing subjective view brought us to the objective view? The answer is both yes and no. We can say *yes*, because God's word is objective in the highest sense. The fact is not merely a subjective state in us, but an *actual event*, an action of God about which he speaks to us through the Bible. Yet, on the other hand, we can also say *no*, because it is not objective in the sense of having nothing to do with us. The gospel is not merely an intellectual doctrine. It is a *message*. In that fact we to whom the message is directed are also subjectively concerned. Only when the message has come to us and been received subjectively has it fulfilled its mission.

In another connection, we have pointed out what the burden of the Christian message is.[3] Here our purpose is only to show that *the fact that the Bible is a message puts the question as to the significance of biblical research for the practical use of the Bible into a new light*. If the Scriptures were only to affect our emotional life, their objective meaning might perhaps be of little importance. But the Bible is a mes-

[3] See p. 4.

sage to us, a message of a divine action which concerns us. Hence it is of utmost importance that the message come to us undistorted, in objective correctness. The message is indeed to affect our subjective state, that is true. But if the content of the message is altered from the meaning of him who sent it, its effect on our subjective life will be false. The objective truth of the message is therefore the basis for its intended subjective effect. Hence it follows that we must earnestly ask just what God's word to us is and in what way it comes to us and is received by us. Here we must not let ideas and theories which we prefer prejudge how God ought to proceed when he would speak to us. We must conscientiously seek to learn how he did proceed. In other words, we must take the Bible just as it is, for there we have the fact at issue.

How, then, does God proceed when he speaks to us? Answer: he speaks to us in plain, ordinary human words such as we find on the scriptural page. But since God has chosen to speak to us in human words, it is his will that we give heed to the human meaning of these words. Only in this way will he meet us. Only in this way do we receive his message.

It is common to encounter a view which asserts that if the Bible is God's word, it is not man's word; that it cannot be both. It is therefore vain to search for the original historical meaning of the Scriptures. When the scholar brings his curiosity to the Bible, he wanders far from the word of God; for God's word cannot be dealt with as one deals with human words. It is not our concern just what these words originally meant. The only thing that concerns us is what God would say to us now by these words; and that, no research can tell us.

Against such a position it must be said emphatically that it is by no means a matter of indifference what the literal meaning of God's word is. It would be impossible to give too much care and labor to the investigation of the proper meaning of the words. He who says that prayer and worship are the unerring means to the correct understanding of the word of God, intending to set them over against earnest study of the objective context in which the word is used, is on the wrong track. Prayer and devoutness do not guarantee that one comes to the true meaning of the word. Subjective piety is not enough. Who could deny that there was much genuine piety in the Catholic church in the Middle Ages? Nevertheless men lost the true meaning of the divine word. Or—to give another example—why did not the Jews accept the gospel of Christ? It was not because they lacked earnestness and zeal. Paul says, "I bear them witness that they have a zeal for God, but it is not enlightened. For, being ignorant of the righteousness that comes from God, and seeking to establish their own, they did not submit to God's righteousness" (Rom. 10:2-3). The correct insight into the word of God is not unimportant. Precisely because it is a message, it is all-important that it come to us with the very meaning which God intended. But one does not come to that insight without earnest labor.

It ought not to be necessary to assert this in the church of the Reformation. The Reformation was engendered not by subjective piety, but by true and deep penetration into the objective meaning of Scripture. There was no one who penetrated so deeply as Luther into the correct meaning of the word of Scripture. No other was so fearful of subjective and arbitrary interpretations. His earnest search for the Bible's objective meaning was crowned with the rediscovery of the gospel, which had been clouded and distorted. One ought not to prejudice the case against honest biblical research by calling it the "vain curiosity" of the scholar. That which constrains the scholar to search the Scriptures is something quite different from curiosity. The Bible has a message for us; but we shall never learn what it is from our own subjective state. It is the objective word that tells us. To come to clear understanding of that message is supremely important for the Christian and the church. When one people, engaged in mortal combat with another, receives a message from the latter offering peace, what is crucial is not their feelings and subjective state, but the terms which the message actually proposes. It is the same with the Bible. When God sends his message to us, when he offers us a covenant of peace, our prime business is to listen to what he says to us. Man shows God small honor when he is more interested in his own subjective state than in what God says.

A kind of fundamentalism is abroad. It is characteristic that it holds rigorously to the literal word torn from its context, indifferent to the objective sense of the passage. It thinks it glorifies the word of God by denying the human element in that word. It objects to submitting the question of meaning to any objective test. It acts as if Scripture has no consistent, objectively demonstrable meaning. And it supports its own interpretation by appeal to the Spirit's illumination and to its own spirituality. Here is clearly another case of laying the stress on one's own subjectivity.

Such indifference to the objective content of the word rests ultimately on a view that is alien to Christianity, on the religion of the natural man. For Christianity's contest with the religion of the natural man comes to light clearly in the struggle between the objectivity of the word and human subjectivity. It is evident that for the religion of the natural man the stress must rest on one's own subjectivity: one's achievements; one's own feelings, piety, and spirituality; one's mystical experience, and so on. The Bible's position is the direct opposite. It brings us the message of what God has done and will do. It speaks of an objective act which God effected in our world, within human history. Because of this basic fact the Christian faith can never be satisfied with anything less than an objective message. As to God's objective act in Christ, as to something which actually happened in our world, the Bible brings us an objective message, a message whose burden can be stated simply and definitely; and it is because of this objective reality that the gospel is the power of God for salvation to every one who has faith.

This struggle between the Christian faith and the religion of the natural man stretches through the entire history of Christianity. It appears in various ways at different times, but the basic contrast is the same, whether the issue of the time is christology, the sacraments, or, as now, the Scriptures. The

fundamentalist outlook is only the latest example of this reli-
giousness of the natural man. It gives expression to the same
error which the church has had to resist on various issues
through the centuries. It is enlightening to see how the battle
was joined on these issues, and how the church has stood for
the evangelical position.

For natural religion it is axiomatic that, if relationship is to
be established with God, it must be on God's own heavenly
level. In all religions men have thought it essential to raise
themselves up by means of sacrifices and meritorious works,
to achieve a relation with God in mystical and ecstatic experience. The gospel shows us another way, the direct opposite
of the former. It pleased God, when he would establish fellowship with us, to come down to our human level. This is
the distinctive feature of Christianity from first to last.

First this truth appears in an utterly basic way in the area
of *christology*. In Jesus Christ God came down to us. He
meets us as a specific man, but such is that Man that we can
say that it is really God who meets us. So Luther's hymn says,

> "Ask ye, Who is this?
> Jesus Christ it is,
> Of Sabaoth Lord,
> And there's none other God."

There is no God except him who came to us in Jesus
Christ, in his concrete human life on earth. But here men
have stepped forward with their ideas and speculations, saying,
"If Christ is true God, he cannot be true Man." In its earlier
centuries the church had to battle valiantly against that distor-
tion of the Christian faith. But the church has always held
firmly that Christ is both true God and true Man, and that
God meets us in his human life on earth.

The same issue is to be seen in the view of the *sacraments*.
In the sacraments it has pleased God to come to us and be
one with us, in, with, and under certain earthly elements. In
baptism—in, with, and under the rite—he grafts us into Christ;
he makes us members of the Body of Christ, branches in

Christ the vine. But here too human speculations take a hand. A false, magical view asserts that if God acts in baptism, the sacramental water cannot be ordinary water; it must have special divine powers. And in the Lord's Supper, in, with, and under the consecrated bread and the consecrated chalice, the Lord Christ gives himself to us, enters into us, and becomes our life. Again false speculation steps in with its doctrine of transubstantiation. It is affirmed that if Christ is actually present in the Eucharist, the bread and the wine must have been transformed into divine substances.

And now the nature of the word of God, of the *Bible,* supplies another example. When God speaks to us, he does not use some boundless, heavenly language. He talks to us in simple, ordinary, human words, such as we use in all of life's other relationships. His words are borne to our ears on sound waves, in the usual manner. He speaks to us in sentences constructed according to laws of grammar. They can be analyzed and the meaning of words and sentences determined. But these human words are at the same time God's words too. In, with, and under these words God expresses his thoughts and his will. But here again men are not satisfied with the facts as set forth by God. The fundamentalist error arises to say, "If the Bible is the word of God, it is not the word of man, nor is it subject to the laws that govern the human language."

Nevertheless the truth is that we shall not understand God's message to us if we do not heed the meaning of the words in which it is expressed. God has couched it in such words, and only in them can we find his meaning—even as he who does not heed the man Jesus Christ never meets God. "There is no other God," as Luther says.

The issue is the same in all these areas. In the Bible, as well as in Christ and in the sacraments, God meets us on our human level. In grace he comes down to our plane. But the natural man objects, retaining his pagan conviction that we can meet God only by rising up to his heavenly level. Such docetism is as objectionable in our view of the Bible as it is in christology or the doctrine of the sacraments. Docetism is Christianity's hereditary foe. Just as Christ did not merely appear to be human (as the docetists in the early church said) but was true man, and just as the water of baptism and the elements of the Eucharist do not merely look like physical realities, but actually are so, and are used by God as means to his purpose, so the Bible does not merely appear to speak in human words, but actually does so. It is precisely in and through such words that God speaks to us. He who does not concern himself about the true and objective meaning of those words thrusts God's own word aside, and substitutes for it his own subjective speculations.

For the evangelical, Christian view, biblical research must consequently have a place of central and urgent importance. The Bible is at one and the same time the church's book and the individual Christian's book. Biblical research, which feels its special mission to be to make clear the content of the message of Scripture, can never be a matter of indifference to the church. The church can never dispense with scientific study of the Scriptures, even though an individual may not need firsthand acquaintance with it, because the pulpit guides him in his understanding of the message. The church must not be content with only the practical use of the Bible in preaching, Bible study, and devotional reading. It must insist on really methodical study of the Scriptures, overlooking no available scientific aids. Every new age stands under obligation to search its way into the content of God's word, by every means possible. Among these, scientific research has a significant contribution to make.

It need hardly be said that the preaching of the church is not expected to change its character with every shift in exegesis. Scientific procedure, by the nature of the case, often gets into a blind alley and offers many a tentative conclusion. And yet, the serious labors of succeeding generations lead to definite results which the church must make her own and without which she cannot fully serve her mission. When research has erred, it must be corrected; and no one is more careful as to that than scientific scholarship itself. It is part of scientific procedure that it exposes its results to the fires of criticism, by which weaknesses are gradually burned away. But even major errors of science may serve the cause of truth in the long run.

Let one example suffice. What would be the situation now if there had been no study of comparative religions? The fact that contemporary biblical research has led to truer and fuller grasp of the meaning of the gospel is due in large measure to facts to which the study of comparative religions gave emphasis. That study, it now appears to us, made false use of much of that material. It was too often satisfied with hasty analogies which obscured rather than discovered the distinctive character of Christianity. One might therefore think that such study would be a disservice to the understanding of the Christian faith; and so indeed it did seem to many for some decades. But in the longer perspective and in the larger compass of scientific method, it actually led to positive and important results. To be sure, an earlier theological period, the day of "liberal" theology, let its bias lay hold on certain aspects of Christianity which seemed to harmonize with the modern cultural concepts. And comparative religion busied itself chiefly with the aspects least familiar to us. These it set forth in a way that raised questions about how much Christianity could mean to us in our day. But the fact that these very characteristics were thus brought to our attention became the occasion for Christian gratitude. These aspects, which at first seemed strange and troublesome, have served to set forth the Christian message in its tremendous greatness and glory. Now, in a way that was formerly quite impossible, we can speak of the new age and the eschatological hope. We now see better how a regnant secularism stands in the way of a true understanding of Christianity. We have been helped to a truer comprehension of the apostle Paul's statement that God has revealed his righteousness through Christ. All these truths are now living realities, not just dogmatic statements. How did that happen? Not through miscellaneous reading of the Bible, but through a methodical, objective search for the meaning of Scripture with no other purpose than to give clear statement of the facts. God has used the objective study of the Bible, and even the many false steps of the study of comparative religions, to bestow new gifts on the church.

But if biblical research is to yield such results, no external limits may be set to its investigations. Its results must not be bound to predetermined positions, nor its task arbitrarily circumscribed. It is occasion for neither scorn nor objection, when research concerns itself with purely historical problems. That is part of its task. It would be easy enough to show how isolated historical investigations have shed light on the central message of Scripture. For all its apparent insignificance, such research may supply the very details needed to bring separate facts into an inclusive order.

Both the church and the individual have very great reason to be thankful for the help that biblical research has given to clear understanding of the meaning of the Bible's message. Nothing else can contribute as much as honest biblical research to the exposition of the word of God in all its objective majesty.

For Further Reading

By Anders Nygren:

Agape and Eros. Translated by Philip S. Watson. Philadelphia: Westminster, 1953.

Christ and His Church. Translated by Alan Carlsten. Philadelphia: Westminster, 1956.

Commentary on Romans. Translated by Carl C. Rasmussen. Philadelphia: Muhlenberg, 1949.

Essence of Christianity. Translated by Philip S. Watson. Philadelphia: Muhlenberg, 1961.

The Gospel of God. Translated by L. J. Trinterud. Philadelphia: Westminster, 1951.

"Love," in The Encyclopedia of the Lutheran Church. Edited by Julius Bodensieck. Philadelphia: Fortress, 1965. Vol. II, pp. 1345-47.

By other authors:

Richardson, Alan, and Schweitzer, Wolfgang. Biblical Authority for Today. Philadelphia: Westminster, 1951.

Bring, Ragnar. How God Speaks to Us: Dynamics of the Living Word. Philadelphia: Muhlenberg, 1962.

About the method of Anders Nygren:

Watson, Philip S. "Theologians of our Time: VIII. The Scientific Theology of Anders Nygren," The Expository Times, 74, 10 (July, 1963), 300-04.

Wingren, Gustaf. Theology in Conflict: Nygren—Barth—Bultmann. Translated by Eric H. Wahlstrom. Philadelphia: Muhlenberg, 1958. Especially pp. 3-22 and 85-107.

Erling, Bernhard. Nature and History: A Study in Theological Methodology with Special Attention to the Method of Motif Research. "Studia Theologica Lundensia," 19. Lund: Gleerup, 1960.

Johnson, William Alexander. On Religion: A Study of Theological Method in Schleiermacher and Nygren. Leiden: Brill, 1964. New York: Humanities Press, 1966.

Facet Books in Print

220
N99

61369

12. *Kerygma, Eschatology, and Social Ethics*
    by Amos N. Wilder. 1966
13. *Affluence and the Christian*
    by Hendrik van Oyen (translated by Frank Clarke). 1966
15. *Christian Decision in the Nuclear Age*
    by T. R. Milford. 1967
16. *Law and Gospel*
    by Werner Elert   (translated by Edward H. Schroeder).
    1967